BREADTH FOR A DYING WORD

T0363619

Also by Tom Petsinis

POETRY

The Blossom Vendor
Sonnets: Offerings from Mount Athos
Inheritance
Naming the Number
Four Quarters
My Father's Tools

FICTION

Raising the Shadow
The French Mathematician
The Twelfth Dialogue
The Death of Pan

DRAMA

The Drought
The Picnic
Elena and the Nightingale
Salonika Bound
Hypatia's Circle

BREADTH FOR
A DYING WORD

POEMS

TOM PETSINIS

ARCADIA

© Tom Petsinis 2013

First published 2013

Arcadia, the general books' imprint of

Australian Scholarly Publishing Pty Ltd

7 Lt Lothian St Nth, North Melbourne, Vic., 3500

TEL: 03 9329 6963   FAX: 03 9329 5452

EMAIL: aspic@ozemail.com.au WEB: scholarly.info

ISBN 978-1-925003-28-4

Design and typesetting Sarah Anderson

Printing and binding Tenderprint Pty Ltd

Cover artwork Alexia Petsinis

CONTENTS

NOUNS

Stone 2

Coin 3

Canvas 4

Advice 5

Thesis 6

Tense 10

Ornithology 11

Whims 12

Harbingers 13

Poplar 14

Necessity 15

Conversions 16

Antiques 17

Transformation 19

Rhymes 23

Sound 25

Ophthalmology 26

Heart 27

Silence 28

Captive 29

Inheritance 30

Courtyard 31

Home 37

Escape 38

ADJECTIVES

Wishful 40

Totemic 42

Nocturnal 43

Young 44

Unseasonable 45

Faithful 46

Sacrificial 47

Temporal 49

Cthonic 54

Frugal 55

Autumnal 57

New 58

Ocular 59

Tribal 60

Reflective 61

Natural 65

Fearful 66

Primal 67

Centrifugal 69

Passionate 70

Ideal 71

Embodied 72

Purgatorial 73

Seasonal 80

VERBS

Reading 82

Inspired 83

Imagined 84

Revived 85

Assay 86

Speculate 87

Protract 88

Question 89

Attuned 91

Hunting 92

Envisage 93

Efface 94

Musing 95

Rocroato 06

Observe 98

Verbalise 99

Articulate 111

Symbolising 112

Deceived 113

Renew 114

Secrete 115

Starring 116

Gaming 118

NOUNS

STONE

In the beginning, before the word,

A stone was slung at the midday sun,

Blinding it to a brother's crime.

Later, it was found by a monk,

Who kept it under his tongue for years,

Until he set it in a mosaic:

The pupil giving the Creator sight.

In time it was shaped by breath,

Cupped in warm hands like potter's clay.

Others soon got wind of it –

A gift for both the wicked and wise.

Now it's lodged deep in the brain –

A thought burrowing beyond memory

For its meaning as metaphor.

COIN

Pluck a lemon from your neighbour's tree
And squeeze its light in a whiskey glass –
Leave the shilling in there overnight.

A drop of olive oil will restore the shine
That brings a dead king back to his name,
Memory to a year divisible by four:

It's summer, you've just turned eight,
And the stolen coin's sweating in your fist
For the watch in the vending machine.

But more than meaning something to you,
Its worth soars because it was minted wrong –
An image for which poets would kill.

CANVAS

Stapled to a golden rectangle
The canvas you carry home
Dazzles with white's possibility –
A mirror that reflects not
The laws of an incidental light,
But the mind's lawlessness.

Your windows are painted black
Against the day's impositions –
Like the dream-inducing night,
A dark room raises images
From the depths of forgetfulness:
A sea made deeper by a yacht,
A sky heightened by a kite.

You think to start when the wind
Whistles through missing teeth –
And then you're a child again,
Delighting in the art of play:
The canvas freed from its frame,
You cut out a rhombus, a triangle,
And run, as if for your life,
Extending summer's magnitude.

ADVICE

Never ask the timeless when:
Your eyes will tire of lettered light,
Words will lacerate the tongue,
Hope will fall from its height.

Yes, it's too late for tomorrow:
Your faith has begun to wilt,
Flesh is crucified to bone,
Passion sinks to gall and guilt.

Look to living with the dark
Now that sleep draws your head:
The embroidered pillow-case
Is soft with dreams of the dead.

Avoid thinking the thought
That sounds the abysmal why:
Remember there's no escaping
If the night should reply.

THESIS

1

An understanding of silence
Must begin with wonder,
Speculation about its origin:
The great god of death,
Or the quiet death of god.

Later, reason will shape
The small, gleaming hook
For catching answers,
Serving them for dinner,
With a few slices of logic.

Science enters the scene
And autopsies a sound
Found sprawled on the road,
After the traffic has gone.

2

But to know silence well,
As a mathematician knows
His annotated texts,
It must be learnt by heart.

Having its own arithmetic,
It can be added, subtracted,
Even divided by itself
To give infinite stillness.

It's all in the approach,
Like one edging toward zero
But never quite touching it –

When the impossible occurs:
The left hand clapping loud
As the circle is squared.

3

Silence has its aesthetic:

The rhythm of timed spaces

In a symphonic score,

The barefoot dance around

A fire crackling with words,

The gestures of tragedy

When fate chains the hero

To his ultimate fall,

Paintings that say nothing

With eloquent colours:

Black snatched from a mouth

In which hopes are buried,

Crimson from a tongue

Before whispering its love.

4

The humanity of silence
Is the word turned to flesh,
Moving through a world
It will never make home.

You sense it fleetingly,
There in the eyes of an infant
Trying to assemble the sky,
Or the blue-veined hand
Consoling a shoulder
Too steep for winter light.

But you feel its presence
In the dead of night,
Looking down on your body
Angled sharply, asleep.

TENSE

Shuffling through dusty lexicons,

You trip on Sanskrit roots gnawed by the wind,

Latin verbs that died with the last emperor,

The decomposing past of an Attic aorist –

Always looking for the unnamed tense

That would overthrow Time's triumvirate.

The great myths, fantasies and faiths,

Arose when language cut its wisdom teeth,

And reason was still intuition at play.

Maybe what you seek lies in make-believe,

Games of grammar, nonsense rhyme:

Yesterday's the scene of tomorrow's crime.

ORNITHOLOGY

You're not an eagle cruising high,

Its beak circumscribing flesh –

Nor a peacock in the royal park

Spreading a symphony of colour

To soothe the migraine of an empress –

Nor a canary in a wrecker's yard

Whose song, structured by the cage,

Draws the morning sun to lunch –

If anything you're the brown sparrow

Twitching over invisible crumbs

Shaken from last night's tablecloth –

Or the bird, the last of its kind,

Which twitters from a wrinkled elm,

Rejoicing in its namelessness.

WHIMS

Still the wind by pointing to a tree
And betting on the number of its leaves:
The outrageous wind, dishevelled,
Rattling dice in lanes, certain of sixes.

Stand the word upright on the page
For the meaning of its hidden side:
The irreverent word, obsessed with play,
Almost encompassing the world.

Stop the will in the dead of night –
Show it the plunge between heartbeats:
The unquestioning will, using skulls
As stepping stones to morning.

HARBINGERS

Harbingers of summer

Come in barely-noticed ways:

A solitary ant trekking

The arctic of a shower base,

Cracking white in its wake –

A fly on the calendar

Preening iridescent wings

For light's ceremony –

A spider's lacy lingerie

Hung from the rose's thorns

To attract sweet sister-bee –

At evening, the cricket,

Creeping amongst roots,

Counting to extend the day.

POPLAR

She's learnt renunciation,
Leaning to the wind as she must:
The highest leaf falls first,
Deepening the universe.

The lowest lets go last –
There's no shame in being bare:
Summer's shimmering gown
Lies loose on the grass.

Shuffling knee-deep in light,
Children bury themselves in sound –
The old gaze from benches
Sixty winters away.

A man in blue overalls
Stuffs a hessian sack with gold –
He'll hide it the garden-bed,
Beneath the lemon tree.

They come, breathing white,
And release the chainsaw's scream:
She hesitates, then falls, as if
Surrendering to love.

NECESSITY

Secure in a solid-brick residence

And versed in the letter of the law,

You'll never feel the necessity

That extends an obliterated palm –

But they've learnt it by heart

Whom circumstance has exiled

Beyond their tongue's peninsular,

To a language barbed with sibilants –

Know the want that crumbles breath

To consonants, vowels, sighs,

Enough to ask for bread and milk,

Tasting the accent's bitterness.

CONVERSIONS

If your sorrow should contract to rock,

May it not become a lump of coal

That makes eyes water with its smoke,

Nor a block of granite polished to a shine,

Engraved with death's golden dates –

But the random stone shot from a sling,

That scattered a menagerie of clouds

At the beginning of the summer holidays.

If your faith should conform to speech

May it not become the hymn sung by all,

Nor the prayer that whispers your fear,

But the word ignited by two lovers

When crimson tongues suddenly touch,

That clears the night, morning mist,

Revealing the mirror of a mountain lake,

Echoing the circle of a pebble's fall.

ANTIQUES

Arms angled sharp on the counter
Prop your head heavy with memories.
Smoking helps loosen knotted thoughts –
Wispy threads unwind, fill the shop.

You're defined by this mix of things
Which neither natural selection
Nor a Creator could've assembled –
You love the charm of chaos or chance.

The photo of those fading debutantes –
Serrated edges nibbled by time –
Goes back to when hearts wanted more
Than bare hands could ever hold.

The company of clocks on the back wall
Raced off to the future years ago –
Their outline remains, and grandfather,
Tapping, upright in his coffin.

Silverware in purple reveals its age,
Books are brown with nicotine.
Not what they used to be, mirrors
Can't ricochet your smile to infinity.

A young couple buys a bedroom lamp,

Winking that your prices are a steal.

Their bright presence redeems your past –

The old cash register rings loud, last.

TRANSFORMATION

1

The combinations were infinite,

But after each failure you reasoned:

As mud had given shape to man

And water changed to wedding wine,

The mind would now perform its miracle.

So, forehead closer to the flame,

You lulled mute lead with incantations,

Crushed sulphur in the full moon,

Mixed quick mercury with blood,

Guided by the glow of imagined gold,

Though not for the sake of wealth

(They've overcome possessions

Who seek the philosopher's stone),

But to raise base earth to elemental sun.

Colour is captured by matter's will

(A cup is red only in appearance,

In essence it's the complement of red),

And so you extract it from things:

Black from a diamond's shine,

Blue from a bird's broken egg-shell,

Yellow from daisies yoked to spring,

Green from blades sharpened by wind.

A visionary, emptying your pupils

On canvass, paper, walls plastered white,

You liberate colour to playfulness,

Creating a meaningless masterpiece:

Fruit ripened by integrated light,

Filling the living-room's empty bowl.

3

When pebbles still counted sheep,

You had thought the sensual through –

Freeing the pentagon from its lines

To grasp the eternal beauty within,

Stripping back even music's charm

To the silence of bare arithmetic.

With dishes raised to a generous sky,

You now number their collections,

Abstracting formula from fact

To measure the curvature of space,

The distance to the penultimate prime.

Tomorrow, having digitised all,

You'll pass it through mother-matrix,

Contracting the universe to a point.

4

Echoing the Big Bang's infant hum,

Language resonates through space,

Giving rise to a host of natural things,

And thought-expanding alphabets.

You seek the word in its worldly form,

Hoping to find its original source –

The word, perhaps a single sound,

The key to unlock 'light', 'sea', 'stone' –

Perhaps a line, a lyric, an epic poem,

Which, when recited by heart,

Would draw you to the creator's thought –

Or perhaps the organ's last note,

Absorbing in a swell all that went before,

Making your body lighter than soul.

RHYMES

You aren't louder, open mouthed,
And crying full the nursery:
Twilight grazes the head of clown
Pale at what he doesn't see.

You aren't faster, crawling still,
Reaching for the distant train:
Hare-heart's racing up the hill,
Pursued by a barking pain.

You aren't braver, facing night,
Alone, a captive, in a cot:
Before coming for your sight
Darkness takes the dice's spots.

You aren't taller, hoping high,
Flying on a rocking horse:
This is how myths arise,
Lots of playful metaphors.

You aren't younger, staring hard
At the mirror and the clock:
You catch your laughter in the yard
And keep it in a money box.

You aren't lesser, lacking words,

Even as they talk and talk:

You draw the outline of a bird

With blue, spit-softened chalk.

SOUND

A score grows from a sound:

The blind clock, picking concrete,

Taking a shortcut to the future,

Or twigs snapping in the winter dark –

These become the symphonies

That warm hands with applause.

A tune grows from a heartbeat:

Remembering your first love,

Sighs suppressed by collar and tie,

The breath that buries your name –

These become the melodies

That lighten bodies with dance.

OPHTHALMOLOGY

There's not a spot of summer
In a film of cataracted pupil,
Only the sun's permanent eclipse
Frozen in the cell's nucleus.

Magnified a thousand times,
There's no trace of a dream
In the crystal cornered by sleep,
Only light's rigid scaffolding.

Even an electron microscope
Can't find a hint of sorrow
In a drop taken from a tear-duct,
Only the geometry of salt.

Dispensing with instruments,
You stare into the convexed eye
Until it shines with images
And begins weeping for you.

HEART

When heart first sang, you raged,

Cursing that it couldn't fly away.

Wisdom comes with a touch of grey:

The song's perfected in the cage.

Later, punting daily at the pub,

You'd spur heart first past the post.

But overnight it became an ox

Yoked to creaking bones by knots

Of sinews, carting off a host

Of carnivals with a plodding thud.

With less time, life diminishing,

You began to think, calculate,

Counting the throbs in your wrist,

Avoiding the stillness between.

Now you feel what nothing means:

Heart's contracted to a fist,

Bruised from pounding the gate

Numbered with the sign of infinity.

SILENCE

Whether it's a science or an art
A disciplined study of silence
Always starts with an open mind –
Wonder verging on reverence.

Do dreams feed the multitude?
Reason twists reverence to a hook
And casts it in a shining arc –
The answer begs a slice of moon.

In itself a force is mutely one,
A formula memorised from texts,
Not lemons dropping in the dark,
Nor the groan of a nuclear test.

When a leaf's carefree fall
Makes the forest hold its breath,
Space rises, ripples, expands
To embrace both galaxy and flesh.

Finally, when all speech fails
And the patient can barely nod,
Silence drips its humanity
As the respirator hums of God.

CAPTIVE

Confined by the of strictures of bone

You'll never run free looking for words

Pressed by a desiccating page –

Defy old age, pursue the thieving wind,

Retrieve the tune it snatched from your lips,

Dance around the expurgated song.

Sentenced to life, solitary in a skull,

You'll never see light calculating its speed –

Learn from the innumerate dream:

Soften with spit a handful of yellow clay,

Warm it in the hollow of your palm –

It will rise from the darkness and shine.

Caught in the grip of another winter

You'll never grow wings staring at trees –

Step out in slippers crushed at the heel,

Gather the twigs discarded by birds.

The flames will lick your extended hands

And your imagination will soar.

INHERITANCE

Finally, when it's read aloud,

The will that promised the world

Always cheats the loyal child.

This is your real inheritance:

Stones that extended the horizon,

A creek crying like a lamb,

Wheat fields full of sunken gold,

Bare knees grazed by twilight,

And then the white-washed house

Retreating from the coming dark,

Gathering the moonlit path,

The courtyard, shoes, doorstep,

Until everything's safe and sound,

Here in the room of your birth.

COURTYARD

1

Brother bluestone was versed in propriety:
Prison walls ran straight, churches rose to a point,
Angled gutters kept water moving in lines,
Back lanes were short-cuts between bookie and pub,
Spikes in the cemetery fence subdued desire.

But something more subtle was needed here:
Sister sandstone was quarried by bare-armed men,
Caressed, smoothed, carted like a bride
To this waiting space, which she soon embraced
As arch, turret, tower with a four-faced clock.

A cloister for minds bowed to logic and law,
From cosmic winds scattering the stars –
This courtyard, centred (as if by an afterthought)
On a Moreton Bay fig instead of the flag.

2

The only season here is the yellowing text,
The only emotion a yearning for justice not joy.
Snarling from above, gargoyles frighten off
Red-breasted swallows gathering twilight and twigs,
Silencing a young couple awkwardly in love.

Stale light spills from the library's windows,
The bored attendant's yawning for a lawless night,
A girl in flared jeans, with legs crossed twice,
Is looking for the Act governing dreams.

The last moot's finished in lecture-room one:
Tomorrow's barrister has folded his shadow in eighths,
The judge is groomed, already wiser than white,
Students emerge, subdued, head-deep in thought.
The tree whispers earth's perennial truth.

3

Deaf to a dry leaf scraping on bitumen,
A cricket struggling with the names of dead stars,
The physicist experiments with paper and pen,
Calculating the curvature of infant space.

Mathematics is selfless, eternally young,
Knowledge for the sake of just wanting to know,
Inspiring him to take the quantum leap
Over the dreadful abyss between zero and one.

There's no need of hope or heaven in the lab –
Death starts only when numbers run out of breath.
He bows to his silver instruments in faith,
Accounting for the error that comes with each,
Until consciousness accelerates to the speed of light,
Becoming infinite at once, theoretically a soul.

4

In an office with curtains partly drawn,
The Head of Philosophy stares into a short black,
Smoking metaphysics down to the butt.

He thinks best alone, as evening descends,
(The young secretary's perfume was far too strong) –
Thinks of a tree with more branches than leaves,
A sun that's said in less than one syllable.

Above, in the white bowl hanging from a cord,
A moth blinded by proximity to light
Flutters madly in the grave-yard of its kind.

He is thinking of what thought might become:
Will driving hard to push through that wall of books,
To break cause and effect, crack open the skull,
Fly to where knowing and being are one.

5

Watchful in the tower crowned in bronze,

Time, the assassin, hiding behind Roman numerals,

Striking the student running late for the future.

Time, the guardian, hands above suspicion,

Who gives the sun daily its round loaf of bread,

The moon its monthly wage of silver coins.

Time, the tutor, teaching young hearts to count,

But never backwards to the beginning,

Who sets strict dead-lines for compulsory assignments

And grips girls for the throb in their wrist.

Time, a phantom force, now tolling the hour,

The sixth and last quivering through the winter dark,

Expanding, a circle embracing the courtyard,

Blocks of sandstone dissolving like sugar cubes.

6

Centred at the crossing of exits and entrances,
The tree has flourished a century or more,
Offering book-hugging bachelors generous shade,
Refuge to fidgety sparrows, movement to stone,
Shedding its gold joyfully each year.

This morning, the first of another spring,
Their calculations done, men are drilling into dry sap,
Bracing sagging branches, bolting them with rods,
Defying gravity with crutches and stakes.

But it has long outlived its Latin name,
Learning by degrees to release its hold on light,
To stop counting the dark rings in its trunk.

Faculties deny birthright and natural justice,
Insisting death has no place in the shining mind.

HOME

It escapes the alphabet that kills,
Slips through the countless permutations
Of your four-lettered genetic code.
Open your eyes, read your inheritance:
This town centred on a monolith
Whose meaning has darkened to moss,
These houses with grills and gates
Numbered in multiples of five,
A cobbled street named after a god,
This square with statues turning green,
Old men playing chess in the dark.

Each morning, walking to work,
You stop a moment on the stone bridge,
Looking for yesterday's reflection
Carried off by the river flowing south,
Thinking: life's better overseas.
But, as always, you turn and move on,
Following your evaporating breath,
Knowing you'd be nothing there,
A foreign name, lost in translation.

ESCAPE

You manage to escape the word
That penned you to the unforgiving page.
Before you think even half a thought
A reward's out for your capture,
If not your whole body, dead or alive,
Then your eyes, with or without sight.

With little rhyme and less reason
You set out for proof of your innocence.
It's not in basil retreating in green,
Whose scent once promised redemption,
Nor in the girl blossoming a smile,
Breasts budding full to womanhood.

Disheartened you're off to surrender
When it stops your imagination:
A thrush, shimmering on a steeple's cross,
A winter twig in its yellow beak –
The irrefutable proof that will
Vanquish the word, vindicate you.

ADJECTIVES

WISHFUL

If colour could be carried home
Like Friday's fruit in a styrene box,
Though not for its sweetness
But to decorate the living room –
Colour peeled thin as light,
(Leaving flesh to delight the tongue)
And placed on a broad palette
For mixing as nature never dreamt –
What exotic tastes you'd excite.

If sound could be timely cut
By scissors crossing in degrees,
Not just the lengths of practiced notes
And their surrounding silences,
But the rattle of the busker's can
And discord plucked from wired streets –
Cut and stored in earwax
Until necessity prevails –
What symphonies you'd score.

If hands versed in private reason

Could gather the tooth-marked letters

Scrabbled on the polished floor

And glistening with a child's saliva –

Gather them in speechlessness

As a cubic alphabet, nothing more –

What a language you'd create,

Not only for expressing wishful thoughts

But to communicate with all.

TOTEMIC

As a thing thought out in full

The elm's not a trap set in spring

To snatch from its mating call

The bird silent on the wing,

Nor is it meant to net the breeze

Whose thrashing in the dark

Keeps the widow knitting late,

Nor is it the appendage of shade

That draws old men in white

To sit cross-legged and sip tea –

No, the elm's a totem pole,

Intended to keep flighty minds

From what would otherwise be there:

The abyss concealed by a twig.

NOCTURNAL

To sing like a cricket new to song:

Hesitant at first, three false starts,

As though uncertain of its own voice,

Reason for connecting with the dark,

Until it finds its purpose and pitch,

The syncopated count in two-beat time

Perfected by the struggle of its kind,

When its self-confidence outgrows

Its body and span of brittle wings,

The sound waking wonder in a child,

Cracking concrete still warm with sun,

Rising to a crescendo that compels

The dead to pick earth from their ears,

Stars to reverberate and tingle.

YOUNG

Bolder than black
But innocent as the green
Now tickling its back,
It wants to behold
What no shadow's seen.

'This enlightened age
Has opened my eyes.
I'll stop serving the page
And look to the source,
Not afraid to die.'

'You're still young,'
Warns the grey gumtree.
'Restrain your tongue,
Respect what your kind's
Not meant to see.'

Jaws set, will fixed,
It tests the axe's bite
On a thin wrist,
Positioned to sidestep
The falling height.

UNSEASONABLE

You see again the pebbled path

That quickened steps to the future.

How long has it been since

That summer in the magpie's park

When, running between elms,

Your heart counted faster by fives?

How long since you cracked

And bit the kernel of an apricot?

Yes, autumn took you by surprise,

Like the dishevelled derelict

Whose scraping followed you home.

Now you stand in thinning blood

As winter inhabits your breath.

FAITHFUL

It's been hounding you all morning,
Spoiling the long-awaited holiday.

You hoped to lose it at the cemetery,
Crossing the shadow of a cypress tree,
But it scented your soles and stuck
Like bitumen that's just been poured.

You walked on, always facing east.

The sun poised on the tip of twelve –
Now's the instant to try another slip,
Up, this time, past the steeple's point,
A bee-line for the circle of light.

You're falling, unafraid, free at last,
Knowing it will disappear beneath you,
In death's two-dimensional space.

SACRIFICIAL

Restless as a yellow flame,

It filled the underground with song

Sounding its longing for sky,

Its memory of a distant mating call –

Song, as a means to an end,

A tested instrument of change,

Kept close to a rusty lantern's glow

And the glint of picks on stone,

Allaying uncertainty and fear –

Song, that moved men and machines

Through forests of eucalypt

Embracing the meaning of black,

That raised nuggets of night

For the foundry, fireplace, stove.

Wresting wages from the dark,

Softening the rock-face with sweat,

Exchanging coal for corn bread,

Those shades had no feeling

For a small flame fluttering alone,

No time for embroidered trills –

The song was mechanical to them,

Like the tick of an alarm clock

That assures sleepers they're dreaming –

.

Its silence, louder than a siren,

Was the signal to snatch a breath

And scramble from the mine –

The demon that haunted those depths

Going first for the singing throat.

TEMPORAL

1

Moulded by the river's flow
The eel glides with graceful ease
When defying the current,
Weaving back to its beginning.

A product essentially of time
Memory moves against time's undertow,
Against the noisy rush of years,
To a cuckoo echoing its call.

Tails snipping the clear sky,
Beaks shining with pins of light,
Swallows are threading the courtyard,
Patching a childhood with joy.

Your grandmother's in black,
Whitewashing stones hemming the path,
And steps leading to the front door
Stained by the wine of farewells.

The house is ready for Easter:
Marigolds brighten window sills,
The lintel crossed with candle smoke
Is still beyond your fingertips.

2

You've come home at last
From battles crackling in the hills –
Covered in flour for the dead
Hands scold you for forgetting the time.

You always count the seven steps
In climbing up to your room –
Each one's higher than the one before,
With an oleander potted in a tin.

Parents claim you at a glance
From the photo of their wedding day,
The iron bed-end's still marked
From the first bite of your milky teeth.

The kilim on the wall saddens you:
Her cheeks glowing like pomegranates,
The girl's pitcher will never fill
From the square's free-flowing tap.

It's always been in the house,
The clock with a double-headed chime –
Now it springs at you like a trap,
Scaring God in the icon case.

3

Suddenly, caught by its tick,
You become curious at how it keeps
The busy household in line,
Prodding the silence outdoors.

When geese letter the low sky
It accompanies the clattering loom –
Your Mum's feet quick on the pedals,
As though to a dancing tune.

On the longest night of the year
It chips surely through the frozen dark,
Like your Dad's tireless pick
Grinning for limestone and coal.

When it tires, slowing to a limp,
Your grandfather winds it with a song –
Our guide to the future, he says,
And blows out the lamp.

Waiting for dreams to come,
Alone in the silence between breaths,
You're alarmed by the thought:
What happens when the heart stops?

4

The clock pressed to your chest,
You take it out for your Dad to see:
Time flies, he nods, and sighs,
But you don't know what he means.

Later, memorising the moment,
You race to him working in the yard,
Before the circle of numbers
Slips from the tip of your tongue.

The long arm's almost on six
(You say this first because of its size) –
The short, between two and three,
Moves only when no-one's present.

At school, under its discipline,
You learn to count from one to sun,
From nought beyond night –
Knuckles struck red at each mistake.

And soon you master the game,
Riding the second hand, becoming fast
At doing subtractions from twelve,
Racing to sixty in leaps of five.

5

The clock's stopped in its tracks,
Spent from sounding so many seconds –
Your grandfather tried fixing it
With oil from the icon lamp.

Here, find time's soul, he smiles –
And you take it out cupped in your hands,
Like the birds you find in the yard,
Rigid and dead to the bone.

It's yours, a plaything, the first,
Better than the toy-watches in the shop.
You spin the hour-hand back,
Imagining time's in your control.

You raise its face to the sun –
Its shadow inseparable from yours –
Hoping to warm the darkness inside,
Make its soul sound again.

At night, caught in your embrace,
It moves to the even beat of your heart,
Until you slip into timelessness,
Curled tighter than a spring.

CTHONIC

Breath thwarted by tongue and teeth
Set together like when the infant
Draws the world from warm breasts
Sustained and strengthened early man,
Who tamed the terrible with sound.

For blond, blue-eyed Northerners
Emerging from mists thick with thought,
The rose's thorn didn't bite as much,
Thunder wasn't as loud at night,
Earth was lighter on the buried youth.

Greeks grew with myths and maths:
While thanatos tasted of Athenian grapes
And covered a corpse in purple cloth,
They could anthologise their gods,
Sing the theorem of Pythagoras.

Brows leather-bound and darkened
By the silence between aleph and beth,
Jews found their consolation
For the loss of Ruth and Jonathon,
The climb from Bethlehem to Golgotha.

FRUGAL

The ancestral house would've been yours –
But, no, you've chosen this rented room instead,
Whose walls you stripped down to bare plaster,
To feel your shadow in its moment of fear.

Floorboards are love-locked, tongue-in-groove,
And polished monthly by the waxing moon.
Courting nightingales wake you with their song
When dreams go sleepwalking in the dark.

You removed the dead-lock from the door
(Keys anchor the mind they're supposed to free):
Should a thief come for your numbered name
You'd catch him by surprise with a question-mark.

The clock's mute on a pile of unread books,
Paralysed by a stroke a second, or a season ago.
You shattered the mirror, rejoicing in the sound,
Keeping a triangle for grooming the sun.

The table's never for entertaining friends,
But to rest your bruised elbows in contemplating
The flight of birds in its horizontal grain,
A forest's grief in the black-eyed knot.

In the corner where light and shade couple,

Your single bed's more for thinking than rest,

For dreaming than sleep, in which you often dream

Of living daily on less, on nothing but breath.

AUTUMNAL

Watch, be attentive, don't lose your count:
When the golden elm sheds exactly half its leaves,
Snatch a breath from the wind, make a wish –
The leaf that flutters to the ground next
Will scurry off, returning with news of the sun.

Your shadow's becoming thinner each day,
And if it should catch on a nail in the paling fence
Don't be alarmed by the trickle of rust –
Listen, having practiced the scale all summer,
The blackbird's perfected its mating song.

Yes, work has a way of overcoming despair:
Uproot the marigolds that withered in their faith,
Shake the forgiving earth from their roots,
Kindle tonight's fire with their crackling stems –
Old words will spring to life in its glow.

NEW

Leaking light from countless spots,

(Yes, there's a need for total dark)

The old sky was removed sheet by sheet,

Trucked to be recycled by rust.

Cranes raised another in its place,

With fourteen moons and seven suns,

Rectangular clouds, lines of bird flight,

Stars that shine only on demand.

And now you recite its name aloud,

Precisely, timed to a third of a syllable,

The aspirate tickling your palm.

It flutters on the galvanised blue,

Caresses the night riveted with studs,

Delivers the dome to your breath.

OCULAR

Moon-licked, the golden calf glowed,

Raised on bare shoulders by men

Too afraid to see that images

Obstruct the god meant to be invoked,

Who approaches in joy and fear.

The vision of transcending flesh,

At least as old as the first infant's cry,

Is torn from the sleeper's eyes

By those who count the fluttering lash,

Who'd digitise the dream of flight.

Reading twigs scattered by the dead,

You ignore lively swallows

Repairing the hundred-year old house,

Hills spreading their new green

To welcome the illiterate sun.

TRIBAL

Death once had a solitary vowel:
A sound that would circle lips
And open to both the wind and sun.
But the tribe lost it following its fate,
Or left it behind with their gods,
Living without it ever since.

Your mother would rarely say it
(Perhaps to keep it from her child),
And then always in a whisper,
Only when wearing a black scarf:
A syllable half rhyming with the cross
She'd make before the icon case.

Having not thought of it in years,
You're now saying it to the mirror:
Yellowing teeth set in a kind of snarl
Against consolation and hope,
Your smart lips sealing with a smile
The mouth of tomorrow's grave.

REFLECTIVE

The morning mist clears,
Having polished to a shine
The surface of the lake.

Admiring its nakedness,
The sun drops a golden coin
That falls in a blink
To twice its midday height.

A cloud drifting overhead
Leaves a trace of permanence,
Faint as a watermark.

Hair knotted to their twin
Willows sink deeper each day,
A deer bowing to its thirst
Recoils from a predator.

The full moon ripples home,
Followed by her brood
Of bright, twittering chicks.

2

A mix of liquid and light,
The eye as a thing seen,
Rather than an organ of sight,
Reveals another world.

The market's caught still
In a fish's frozen glare,
The bulging stare of a lamb.

Breast-feeding at dusk,
And swelling with tenderness,
The mother's an embryo
In her infant's gaze.

In moments of meaning
The lover is embraced
In the other's blue irises.

If God created flesh
It's for the pupil's gleam –
To apprehend His own image
In suffering and death.

3

Thinner than a shadow
It knows light's geometry,
Reversing left and right.

Having no desire at all,
It stands perpendicular to time,
And midway between
Tomorrow and yesterday.

Its nature's ideal for play:
Breaking, not to bring bad luck,
But to multiply the world,

Ambush the startled sun,
Or, when set facing another,
To ricochet the tennis ball
With infinite regression.

In the end, tired of images,
The mirror's restored to itself
In the cleansing dark.

4

When the mind reflects
It doesn't express light's law,
But a creative urge
Often passing for chance.

Reflection, first as taking in,
Not with cold indifference,
But as a good guardian –

Followed by giving back,
So things will come forward,
Closer than halfway,
Recognising themselves:

Clouds in attitudes of grey,
Thunder in a major chord,
A raindrop in a circle –

And then as a memory:
The dead arising at evening,
Reclaiming their form,
Hands warming on breath.

NATURAL

You set out before daybreak again,

The sledgehammer balanced on your shoulder

Mute, colluding with self-centred gravity.

Your first encounter echoes the Big Bang,

Fills space with the scent of infant stars,

Wakes bluestone from dreaming it's the sun.

A holiday, done with weighing words,

You stroll the beach littered with random things,

Caressing a stray zephyr with a sigh

Until it sniffs your discarded footsteps home.

At night it turns the ink-stained dictionary

And settles on the spelling of its name.

Ancestral shepherds were weather-wise –

But here, with freedom still in looking up,

You herd clouds heavy with metaphor,

Prodding them with a fountain pen

Until they fall in line, almost reasonable,

Waiting to be milked of meaning on the page.

FEARFUL

It's time to open the venetian blind
Angled steep against the longest night:
The stranger's gone from the gate,
Who counted black knots on a cord.

Go, step barefoot on the balcony,
Tear the words rooted to your tongue
Like the lists you couldn't spell
And threw away to start the holidays.

Open your mind, liberate your ideas:
They'll circle the sky, but return
Like the flock bringing home a stray.

Scatter your fears in sweeping arcs,
High to clouds ploughed by lightning –
Tonight you'll reap your reward.

PRIMAL

To know a language from within,
Like this house whose keyhole
You slot first time in the dark,
Whose switch you find at a touch,
Give up your hard-bound books,
Find the source of the word.

Beneath speech's ebb and flow,
There's the force that moves rivers,
That moulded slippery clay,
Making an orifice for the wind
That whistled and whistled,
Until a mouth emerged and cried.

The order that created light
Wasn't a test of what will could do,
But a long, desperate howl
Later deciphered as syllables:
A god's need to be soundly defined
By the scope of the universe.

The necessity that draws a stone
To oneness with its name
Is like the instinct that screams
For the silence of the breast –

Galactic vowels that sustain life

And give the lyric strength.

You know a language to is roots

When torn from your mother tongue

And exiled in speechlessness:

A migrant or refugee

Yearning to be understood,

Extending a lined, eloquent hand.

CENTRIFUGAL

If you could spin your thoughts
As grandmothers worked their yarns,
You'd weave a sea that's all surface,
Where hooks and anchors couldn't sink,
Without separations and death.

If you could spin your thoughts
As the potter's wheel quickens clay,
You'd shape slippery Time differently,
Giving it the urn's curvature,
So there's no beginning or end.

If you could spin your thoughts
As the cyclotron accelerates particles,
You'd go back to the Big Bang
And create a light that wouldn't shadow
The bride on her way to church.

If you could spin your thoughts
Like a juggler twirling coloured rings,
You'd juxtapose random images
Until a dreamscape filled the night,
In which you find your way home.

PASSIONATE

You grabbed light by the hair,

Mixed three parts paint to one blood

When impressions were thin.

Your annual allowance went

On canvasses nobody wanted to see:

Cubes in six dimensional space.

Now, body worn almost to bone,

You pick charcoal from last night's fire

To sketch on whatever you find:

A river flowing against bitumen,

A bare fig tree on a love-stained sheet

Spread across the afternoon,

Flames on a red-brick wall,

And on the back of a discarded mirror

A self-portrait seen from behind.

IDEAL

Necessity confined to a cell,
Waiting for the synaptic switch
That converts zero to one,
Darkness to uncreated light.

It seeks a form all its own,
But not as life claws blindly
Through clay, sap, marrow, blood
To the strongest of each kind,
To sight in a visionary eye –

Not as water feeling secure
In the embrace of whatever it fills,
Nor breath moving words
Toward a definition of soul.

A thought, pure as a point,
Striking migraine deep for release,
That would realise a new space –
A beautiful geometry
Unconstrained by shape.

EMBODIED

The mind is the measure of all things:
An ideal work redeems your failing body
With what Nature fails to perfect.

Disfigured by arthritis your fingers
Once counted syllables that set brumbies
Galloping through water and wind.

Soles tough as hide, arches fallen, flat,
Those purple-veined feet broke new ground,
Marching to your heart's iambic beat.

Your teeth have lost their incisiveness
From years of chewing a maternal tongue,
Gnawing words for the marrow of truth.

A film of milk eclipses those pupils
That once would seize the sun at a glance,
Converting it to dazzling metaphors.

Low as a petty criminal's, just as hard,
Your lined brow can still forge the images
That bribe the illiterate prison guard.

PURGATORIAL

1

Sun screened by polaroids and cream,
Middle-age tied to shoes with double knots,
You time your daily run on the clock
Shining from the cemetery-keeper's residence.

The last lap and your pace quickens
At the scent of cypresses spiking the fence,
The crowded tram grinding the other way,
Names and dates engraved in stone.

You're thinking: there's a poem in this –
When a shadow swoops from a tree,
Going straight for your unprotected breath,
Smothering your senses with darkness.

You struggle, from a feeling you must,
Fingernails that should've been cut yesterday
Scratching at bitumen, until you yield,
Limbs loosening as in a moment of love.

2

What's become of the afternoon sun?
Why have all the trees turned away from you?
Is that crow calling out your name?
Where's the smell of soil coming from?

A moment ago, all muscle and mind,
You were looking forward to a short black,
Finishing the verse with a rhyme,
Sifting hours for the gold of a metaphor.

This seems distant now, another's dream –
The shadow takes the warmth of your wrist,
Clutches what used to be your breath,
Cuts you from the anchor of your heart.

You always ran past the visitors' gates –
Now a woman greets you at the entrance,
Holds up three lighted candles as you pass,
Spills a glass of red in your wake.

3

You're drawn down a pebbled path
Lit by the memory of a childhood moon.
Skeletal pylons shouldering the sky
Murmur the tune of a memorial hymn.

And then you're standing on a jetty,
Confronted by a broad river brooding past,
When a boat appears, flat, more like a barge,
Easing without creasing the surface.

Set in his profile like a figurehead,
A man extends an open palm for your fare.
You've set out unprepared for this –
No watch, no wallet, no identity cards.

You feel around the roots of your tongue,
Among the myths, legends, nursery rhymes,
Until surprised by a silver coin:
The gift from your godfather at birth.

4

Grinning back to his wisdom-teeth,

He unrolls a contour map of the infinite,

Studies a compass missing needle and north,

Then points to a star scratching the dark.

Are you the only passenger aboard?

And what's he transporting in the hold?

The voyage ends before it starts,

As countless constellations flower and fall.

Images of purgatory spring to mind:

Old prints haunting the walls of living-rooms,

Grey souls etched deep with acid's bite,

Infernos caught in three-lined verse.

In the light of a moth-battered lantern,

The boatman raises a mirror to your mouth –

Stripped of words and metaphors

You're naked as a speechless tongue.

5

Fathoming the depth of your dread,
He says you'll unlearn old habits down here:
Unscramble letters, unscaffold sounds,
Uncage truth with smiles not similes.

His breath's a night-breeze in your face:
Living for the gold of essential light,
Not the fake currency of words,
He gathers fuel that sustains the source.

A hatch opens to the cargo in the hold:
Hessian sacks fat with autumn leaves,
The curvature of apricot and peach
Wasted on mouths incapable of praise,

Jars full of bees that served as go-betweens,
Armour shed by cicadas in summer's clash,
Reels of rainbows, bald acorns with caps,
Bundles of yesterdays tied with string.

6

Having piled his cargo on the pier,
He must return upstream for another load,
Or there'll be no day-after-tomorrow,
No future to lead humanity forward.

You follow his boots grubbing the boards,
But he turns, stops you dead-still, one palm
Tattooed with a right-angled triangle,
The other with a circle and cross.

As penance for refracting new light,
For succumbing to the image of what's real,
For bowing to shadows, not the source,
You're here to stoke the furnace of the sun.

Suddenly, lighter by half a breath,
There's a void where your name should be.
He says: identity's an obstacle to truth,
And memory's healed by a dose of eternity.

7

Left half-scaled on big-bolted planks,
A fish howls at heaven frozen in its eyes.
A whiff of sulphur takes you back
To underground drains explored in youth.

What transgression are you guilty of?
What wrong against humanity or home?
What crime witnessed through a needle's eye?
What sin in a long-forgotten dream?

Your questions are like leaded hooks
Sinking in his inscrutable gaze.
A line of figures moves across the horizon,
Silhouetted against a blaze's afterglow.

A life of discipline, devotion to art,
Nights spent honing your metaphoric sight,
Happiness deferred for retirement –
Your thoughts scatter like bats from a cave.

SEASONAL

A magpie's drinking from the fountain,
Honing its beak on the concrete lip,
Eyeing the night growing without song.

Having squandered its wealth of green
On autumn's two-timing ways,
The pin oak's now shivering for its sins.

Evening light's thinning on the desk,
Renouncing its length and line,
Its sharp black lead shadowing things.

The embers in the fireplace are dozing,
Dreaming of red-gums, droughts,
Bushfires calling heaven to account.

Resigned to being, cold in the skull,
You're counterfeiting images,
Needing your music, summer, warmth.

VERBS

READING

The afternoon broods on whether to rain.
Tight-fisted with Time's currency
You avoid the owner's disappointed look
And slip away following your shoes.
Yes, a dozen titles tempted you,
Prices over indelible endearment and name,
But a question undid your decision to buy:
Is this worth blood's double sacrifice?

You hesitate before stepping outside:
The wind's preparing for the coming word,
Sweeping pages torn from a paperback;
Ozone's heady after those musty thoughts;
Lightning rips a sky purple with prose;
Thunder silences volumes with a clap.
The first drop splats your extended palm –
Payment for reading your future in full.

INSPIRED

Mid-winter, deep in the afternoon,
And sunlight cracks the slate-grey sky,
Clears your vision with its gold:

The bookcase shines like a coffin,
The desk reveals its dandruff and dust,
Numbered days glow in black,
Hands shadow the blank sheet as one.

Sharing the liquidambar with a leaf,
A finch sharpens its beak on a branch,
Picks your ears clean with its call:

A hammer echoes an iambic beat,
The wind draws its bow over power lines,
Your urine sings ceramically
From the bowl's disinfected mouth.

IMAGINED

It's not for amorists in suits,

Nor the body that betrays

The soul whispering to wind,

So remove the silver ring

That defines your singleness,

Free yourself from a watch

That cuffs you like a criminal,

Slip out of your aging skin

And stand bare in the light

Until the journey begins:

Across the spine's footbridge,

Over the depths of the heart,

Through the labyrinthine brain

To a word sounding the ocean.

REVIVED

Moving always from west to east,

You follow lines of skeletons,

Never past the finger bone's tip.

Roaming the vast no-man's land

Between 'I' and neighbouring 'am',

You lose the vowel in your name.

Lacerated by a comma's thorn,

Exhausted from circumnavigating

The full stop's island continent,

You crawl from beneath your tongue.

Emptying pupils brimming black,

You say what the printing press stills –

A child, reading aloud again,

Reviving words, mouth to mouth.

ASSAY

You weigh the silent word
Against the breadth of the wind:
It's lighter by a feather –
The one from a pigeon's wing.

You study the silent word
Magnified in a glass of water:
There's only a cavity
And blood clinging to its root

You taste the silent word
With the daring of your tongue:
Like an apple's black seed
It's bittersweet with cyanide.

SPECULATE

Imagine this: a backyard in suburbia,

Apple and apricot whispering to eucalypt,

Midday perched on a bellbird's beak.

You're sitting here, forehead glistening,

Trying hard to recollect last night's dream,

Draw it out, acquaint it with the world.

A child, your dream refuses to leave

Its bedroom scattered with coloured toys,

Refuses for reasons it will never reveal.

And so now you can only speculate:

Does it fear losing its playfulness out here,

Becoming a tired old memory instead?

Is it real only as lashes flutter in sleep,

Like manic moths around imaginary light,

A pale, indefinite shadow otherwise?

You continue trying to coax it outside,

Needing to see it on the light-green grass,

Barefoot, not bending a single blade.

PROTRACT

It was last used in the incongruous 60's,
When blotter lifted the image of your name:
Radiating from a point, these black lines extended
Beyond page, school desk, to curved space,
Embracing the geometry of a younger universe,
Resting breathless where parallels meet.

Expelled from the exploding sun
A ray slips between the blind's angled slats,
Through the swirl of thought and dust,
Looking for meaning and direction
In the physics text left open overnight,
The crack in the protractor's face.

QUESTION

You say your hope's fading,

Well, so is my persistence –

A summer day's not long enough

For the answers we seek.

So, when the moment comes

For our dreaded metamorphosis,

Who'll find more favour

With the great god of flight?

You, who look for meaning

Away from human sweat,

Though cursed by the brutal fact

That eyes find you beautiful?

You, the flowers' celebrant,

Who exchanges their silent vows,

Accepting the golden pollen

That powders your wings?

You, a believer at heart,

Sipping sunset's communion light –

Or I, who look for truth

In the warm body of night?

(But we're bound one to all:

Yes, I'm cursed with a presence

That alerts my still prey.)

I, who risk the killing clap

For a bit of uncovered flesh?

(My inheritance is clear:

The echo of countless right hands

Applauding a tiny death.)

I, who draw my strength

From a drop of dreamer's blood?

Or, my desperate friend,

Have we both been deceived?

I, sharpening my desire

For life's pleasure and pain,

You, distracted, fluttering,

Pursuing the two-timing sun.

ATTUNED

A day spent recycling recollections:
Those blue veins in your father's wrist
When you'd run to unstrap his watch
And press its warmth to your ear.

You persisted, breathing soft and hard,
Changing the curve of lips and tongue,
Until you whistled to the world.

The conch shell on the windowsill
Still echoes the shambling ocean
That loosened your laughter to the wind.

As the record's last track unwinds
To the hole of silence at its core,
You're no more than five, and counting,
From ten backwards to nought.

HUNTING

Strapped to lead's dead weight –
You, with your obsession for game.
You'd exchange summer's gold
For a single metaphoric flash.

There, water shattering in the dark:
The flight of a hunted image
Sensing your approaching thought.

With mind set, taut as a trap,
You bolt the telescopic bullet,
Stunning the nameless with light.

Firing, you're struck at once –
First by the echo's sharp ricochet,
Then by your own reflection
Springing from startled eyes.

ENVISAGE

It's not a megawatted sun

Defining the world with light,

Shadowing the thing seen –

Nor an insatiable eye

Stripping a tree of its form

To fill a pupil's emptiness –

It's the candle kept in case,

Made more receptive to things

By sudden power failure:

The steady, melting gaze,

The yearning for selflessness

That clears crowded space,

Allowing the visible to glow.

EFFACE

And then there's the other night,
The one that gives meaning to absences,
Waiting to be intimately known
Behind features reflected in a window,
Beyond images and metaphors.

At times, thinking about nothing,
Sensing the abyss between heartbeats,
You almost manage to see through
Your face sculpted by light's necessity,
Apprehend the definition of dark –

But a star brighter than the rest
Nibbles at your pupil like a rat's tooth,
Or the moon, slipping from a cloud,
Silvers your lips with its crescent.

MUSING

When teeth bite into an apricot
It's always for the tongue's enjoyment,
Never for what sweetness means.

Reading to catch the criminal,
Quick eyes overlook the comma
Stained with the author's blood.

Shaped by an eternity of sound
The ear curved into an amphitheatre
To echo the vowel's tragic cry.

The hand that colours lip and lash
In answering the morning-mirror's call
Conceals scripted lines in a fist.

Has the word become flesh?
The punting heart places its last hope
On the throw of a spherical die.

RECREATE

Weave a tapestry from silk

For the living-room wall:

A sea exhausted of waves,

Without a grain of salt,

From which the drowned arise

To satisfy their thirst.

Construct a dome from steel

Using a new geometry:

A sky unstained by smoke

And unreasonable prayers,

That assembles the multitude

In the name of one.

Hammer a golden disc

On the anvil of the heart:

A sun that never sets

And has never learnt the time,

That doesn't cast its ash

Behind unsuspecting trees.

Realise a fleeting dream

Despite the authority of sleep:

The sight of a woman

Alone on the ocean's edge,

Folding her shadow

For the coming holiday.

OBSERVE

When eyes are purified by tears
The world appears in a different light:
The cedar in the cemetery glows,
Letters engraved in gold become a name,
A shadow crunches the pebble path.

For some it's the halves of a walnut,
Others compare it to a small cauliflower –
The brain's more a nest of folded flesh
In which unlikely similes hatch.

If the mind could define itself
It wouldn't be a prisoner sentenced to life,
Scratching the years on the skull
As a way of making time more bearable –
Mathematics is its dream of escape.

VERBALISE

1

You search for its skeletal remains,
Shuffling through lexicons yellow with age
Until dawn crackles the venetian blinds.

Another night, still nothing to show,
Except fingertips dry and dark from print,
And your will bent to a question mark.

Looking out from summer's balcony,
Forget the prophecies of cicadas and flies –
Freeways sound a hymn to the future.

The ghostly gum's not what it seems,
But a trap set in emptiness to catch
·The breeze, birds, wondering thoughts.

Sit at the table, think of a sailing ship,
Slaves and convicts crying the same song
As the ocean's accordion swells.

2

The sun has usurped the creator's place,
Banishing the Word, silencing the vowels
That engendered its nuclear might.

Small shadows cower behind pebbles,
Pupils shrivel that question its authority,
Language retreats under the tongue.

A miracle's like a shortcut to an end –
The sun multiplies matter for the masses,
Turning daily needs to insatiable wants.

This solar age is all zeros and ones:
Cyberspace humming, numbering the world,
Storing it on the point of an angel's pin.

Darkness overcomes light's temptations,
Strips God of attributes and names,
Draws you closer to the creative Verb.

3

Collecting old verbs, you're a child again,
Hinging stamps with strange alphabets,
Flying to countries no longer on the map.

You taste them with the tip of your tongue,
Like testing a battery's nipple for the spice
That shone the torch under the house.

You study their shape and etymology,
Like those butterflies pinned in symmetry,
Names more colourful than their wings.

You turn each one, looking for origins,
Like elm leaves veined with embryonic trees
That taught you about gravity and growth.

More than the sum of its lettered parts
The Verb will spring from print's preserve,
Dancing in the union of skeleton and soul.

4

Shaded from the sun by papyrus sheets,
You tracked the footprints of the Ibis,
To the bestiary guarding dynasties of death.

You walked the desert of no-man's land,
Mind purged of images, customs, traditions –
Sky parchment-crisp for a nameless god.

Following the scrawl of Phoenician snakes,
You stepped barefooted on a beach
Where bleached bones rattled in Greek.

After chiselling Roman patronymics,
You sowed your ancestors' wisdom teeth,
From which a new alphabet arose.

Monks caressed it with their calligraphy,
Until it was initiated by the printing press,
Whose love-bites bruised virgin sheets.

5

At times the Verb brushes your brow,
(Or is it the imagined shadow of its flight?)
Leaving an impression of déjà-vu.

Truth's often found in what's left behind:
Litter in the rush of an ambulance,
A cat's paw-prints in a concrete path,

Circles measuring the depth of a pond,
A budding branch waving good-bye to a bird
That sprang for tomorrow's mating call,

The scent of a letter with a forward slant,
A dream, too subtle for reasoning,
Retreating from the smell of toast burnt black.

It's too elusive for logic and intellect,
But you sense it in the wonder it evokes,
And then always just after it's fled.

6

If God as prime mover is your guide,
Then the Verb you seek is a monosyllable,
And seven-lettered for an active mind.

Like a word that's fossilised in stone
(An epitaph to its own meaning)
You ponder the Verb's motion in space:

A sound that says volumes in a breath,
That rolls the rock from the tomb's mouth
Through the power of resonance alone –

An echo, like that sought by Cabbalists,
Extracting from silence the tone and pitch
That would deliver gold from mute lead.

Perhaps born of space divided by time,
The Verb commences with a sibilant:
A snake's tongue flicking at the speed of sin.

7

What if the Verb's an imaginary truth,

Spun by a mind that turns figures to fantasy,

The matter-of-fact to metaphor,

Or something like the phantom force

That ribbed you riding the merry-go-round,

And moves your shadow as you walk?

Does it exist between cause and effect,

Like the idea of energy that compels

Mass to couple with the velocity of light?

More elusive than the electron's ghost,

Is it also as ambiguous, uncertain,

Vacillating between a process and point,

Now swelling to a wave without end,

Now contracting to a drop from its spay,

Both here and there, thought and thing?

8

Breathing is the will's need to know –
And so you enter another time and place,
When verbs circled the sun with stones.

You follow ancestors whistling their joy,
Harvesting barely for bread and beer,
Gathering winnowed grain in maternal laps –

Using language only when they must,
Preserving words under their still tongues,
Like vegetables in vinegar and salt –

Hunting with hounds scenting a vixen's fear,
With hawks, sight honed by leather hoods,
Eyeing a pigeon's iridescent throat.

The Verb saved for the annual festival,
Like the song passed on from parent to child,
The dance that makes the many one.

9

Language sustains us with possibility:
Nourishing imagination with metaphors,
The heart with parables and myths.

Seen as a field, it's been overused,
The harvest increased for the global market,
Processed, packaged for consumption

In bite-sized blocks, easy on teeth and jaw,
But with wholesomeness diminished,
Vitality dulled, sense and subtlety lost –

Proliferation at meaning's expense:
Words digitised, twittered, texted, blogged,
Glossed to stimulate lust and greed.

Is the Verb threatened by this deluge?
Can you avoid the growing sludge?
Pull yourself out by the tip of your tongue?

10

Unconstrained by objects of desire,
The Verb won't be conscripted by the press,
Nor serve to make policies and profits.

Selfless, it eschews all wishes and wants,
Remaining intransitive to latest trends,
Preferring the freedom of disembodied will:

The long jump's parabolic trajectory
Calculated from an athlete glazed in black,
Hands weighted, thrust forward in flight –

The idea of action on an empty stage,
Or the deftness of the quick-step
Lifted from scuff marks on a polished floor –

Flying, unwinged from a one-legged gull,
Galloping, from a horseshoe nailed to a wall,
Crying, from a creek lost in the dark.

11

Knowledge comes from the unknown,
So you continue, rejoicing in coincidence:
A biblical silverfish obliterating God.

And if the Verb's essentially spirit,
Maybe it's apprehended best through faith:
Devotion, vigilance, a retreat in silence,

Like the saint, knees grinding on stone,
Repeating *Kyrie Eleison* with lips sealed dry,
Behind clenched teeth, under his breath,

As though a forty-day fast from speech,
A cleansing of mouth and tongue
In preparation for the holiest of words:

The Verb that says 'Let there be life',
Quickening your heart to this spring night
Scented with blossom and bitumen.

12

The Verb that says 'Let there be love',
Moving a mother's tireless hands
In making her daughter's wedding dress –

That says, smiling, 'Let there be death'
As a student-nurse times an old man's pulse,
A lively watch pinned to her breast –

That swells your lungs, fills your breath,
And says in less than a syllable
What an expanding universe must fulfil –

That says, through being, 'Let there be',
Suckling galaxies on a new mother's milk,
Compressing eternity between palms –

The Verb that rises from its skeleton
To say, rhyming with every sound,
To sing the marriage of matter and mind.

ARTICULATE

The need that furnishes a room

Fills the closed mouth with speech.

The cry that wakes the world

Draws the breast swollen with vowels

That nourish the melodic line,

Strengthen language to its teeth.

The word that exploded the dark

Wasn't a show of godly will,

But the sigh of someone being alone:

A need to be housed soundly

Not only in bluestone and knotted oak

But in humour and hymn.

SYMBOLISING

The dark boat sank without trace,

The scythe crumbled from scabs of rust,

The angel flew off beyond belief –

Each age has its symbol for Death:

A black hole devouring galaxies

Like milky sweets cellophaned in light

Instils cosmic wonder, not fear.

Like rivers, reapers, beating wings

It's also rich in poetry and play:

With gravity stronger than the grave,

It can shrink the sun to the size of a pupil

Dazzled by a nuclear holocaust,

Intimate an afterlife parallel to this,

Where heaven and hell finally cross.

DECEIVED

You've exposed the old deceit:
Your dreams were squandered on daylight,
Lured by the promise of its gold.

A gatherer of recyclable scraps,
You now scavenge the streets of suburbia,
Sensing potential in everything:

A rainbow's arc in an oil slick,
The hour's butt-ends crushed in a corner,
A computer missing its memory.

Working at night, always alone,
You sift and sort, combining this with that,
Assembling images for dreams.

RENEW

The season's buzz has darkened,

Its wax deep in crimson ears.

Autumn light finer than gauze

Binds two hands together as one.

A child's first word catches on

The thorns of the backyard rose.

At sunset a crow sounds its joy

As pin-oaks blaze in their leaves.

The moon's honed to a crescent

On the front door's bluestone step.

Grandmother Night comes early,

Sowing pupils with marigold seeds.

SECRETE

The snail crushed on concrete
Forgives the footstep in the dark,
Leaving its legacy behind:
A trail gleaming in moonlight,
On which a lost generation
Will make its way home.

Worn black by widowhood,
Her needles crossed in hope,
The spider has spread her grief
In the dead of night:
A net not for sustenance
But to catch the morning sun.

Sinewed to flesh and bone
You sigh when a cricket sings
Another day to stone:
The dead arise at twilight
And walk barefoot to your eyes
Along a dry tear stain.

STARRING

A star that died a stone-age ago

Is the certainty of these pebbles

Worn knuckle white by water and wind,

And children's number games at dusk:

Picked from a path now sealed in bitumen,

They break their silence with a kiss –

Spicing the night with nitre and sparks.

A star that died before the first spring

Is the appearance of this blossom

Staring at the darker side of life and leaf:

Snipped by young girls walking past

And scattered like pink confetti,

Or stripped from limbs by lashing rain –

It falls in gutters as fruitful sacrifice.

A star that died a night-time ago

Is the observation of an eye

Dazzled by a sun it can't comprehend.

Neither flesh nor fully fluid,

But still evolving to the stuff of light,

The pupil is a perfect circle

Open to the sky's chandeliered dome.

A star that died three thoughts ago

Is the flash of an unexpected metaphor

That leaves lightning dead in its wake.

Like the three-lettered formula

That equates momentum and mass,

It also alliterates the beginning

With what you'll eventually become.

GAMING

The sun casts the same shadows as yesterday,

The same wind follows you down the dead-end lane,

Tickets torn with the same anger litter the entrance,

The walls are lettered with the same luckless love.

The stairs to the basement are wooden, worn,

Constructed to block feet from going the other way.

For a moment you imagine they're marble,

Spiralling upward, vanishing to a point of light.

Halfway down, hope catching on a nail-head,

You stop for your heart limping three steps behind.

A fierce bulb keeps the darkness in a corner.

The steel door opens at the whisper of your name.

The mirror greets you, cracks your reflection,

Throws it back in your face like worthless currency.

Numbered in black the clock's been timeless for years,

Its arms with the moths at the bottom of the case.

The patrons are mute, fixed in their profiles,

Pale as the outline of where a calendar once hung,

Deaf to the rattle of dice, blind to the flash of an ace –

All recollecting, reliving, the bet of their life.

A burnt match between his gold-crowned teeth,

The dealer nods to a chair you've sat in countless times.

The cards are shuffled, cut, and dealt out in pairs –

Your losing hand evokes the same surprise.